BEARPORT BIOGRAPHIES

CHADWICK BOSEMAN

ACTOR AND ACTIVIST

by Rachel Rose

Minneapolis, Minnesota

Credits

Cover and Title page, © Michael Kovac/Getty Images; 4, © Krikkiat/Shutterstock; 5, © Emma McIntyre/Staff/Getty Images; 7, © Paul Bruinooge/Contributor/Getty Images; 8, © EQRoy/Shutterstock; 9, © NurPhoto/Contributor/Getty Images; 11, © Sean Pavone/Shutterstock; 12, © Stuart C. Wilson/Stringer/Getty Images; 13, © Ga Fullner/Shutterstock; 14, © Alberto E. Rodriguez/Staff/Getty Images; 15, © TM/ROT/Capital Pictures/MEGA/Newscom/UCGBR/Newscom; 16, © Paul Archuleta/Contributor/iStock; 17, © LeoPatrizi/Getty Images; 18, © Tommaso Boddi/Stringer/Getty Images; 19, © Kevork Djansezian/Stringer/Getty Images; 20, © Brian Stukes/Contributor/Getty Images; 21, © Kathy Hutchins/Shutterstock

Bearport Publishing Company Product Development Team

President: Jen Jenson; Director of Product Development: Spencer Brinker; Senior Editor: Allison Juda; Editor: Charly Haley; Associate Editor: Naomi Reich; Senior Designer: Colin O'Dea; Associate Designer: Elena Klinkner; Associate Designer: Kayla Eggert; Product Development Assistant: Anita Stasson

Library of Congress Cataloging-in-Publication Data

Names: Rose, Rachel, 1968- author.
Title: Chadwick Boseman : actor and activist / Rachel Rose.
Description: Minneapolis, Minnesota : Bearport Publishing, [2023] | Series: Bearport biographies | Includes bibliographical references and index.
Identifiers: LCCN 2022041573 (print) | LCCN 2022041574 (ebook) | ISBN 9798885094016 (library binding) | ISBN 9798885095235 (paperback) | ISBN 9798885096386 (ebook)
Subjects: LCSH: Boseman, Chadwick--Juvenile literature. | African American actors--Biography--Juvenile literature. | African American political activists--Biography--Juvenile literature. | LCGFT: Biographies.
Classification: LCC PN2287.B645 R67 2023 (print) | LCC PN2287.B645 (ebook) | DDC 791.4302/8092 [B]--dc23/eng/20220915
LC record available at https://lccn.loc.gov/2022041573
LC ebook record available at https://lccn.loc.gov/2022041574

Copyright © 2023 Bearport Publishing Company. All rights reserved. No part of this publication may be reproduced in whole or in part, stored in any retrieval system, or transmitted in any form or by any means, electronic, mechanical, photocopying, recording, or otherwise, without written permission from the publisher.

For more information, write to Bearport Publishing, 5357 Penn Avenue South, Minneapolis, MN 55419.

Contents

Red-Carpet Night 4
Book Lover, Story Lover 6
On-Screen Inspiration 10
Off-Screen Superhero 16
Celebrating Chadwick 20

Timeline 22
Glossary 23
Index 24
Read More 24
Learn More Online 24
About the Author 24

Red-Carpet Night

It was a big night for Chadwick Boseman. Cameras flashed as he stepped onto the red carpet at the world **premiere** of the superhero movie *Black Panther*. He folded his arms across his chest, just as his character does in the film. This greeting had become a way to **celebrate** Black culture. His fans let out a huge cheer.

Black Panther broke records, making over $1 billion in its first month in theaters.

Book Lover, Story Lover

Chadwick was born in Anderson, South Carolina, on November 29, 1976. He grew up in a home filled with books. Chadwick was interested in reading about Black history. He was **inspired** by stories of people from the past. Soon, Chadwick started watching stories told on stage, too. He developed a love for theater.

Growing up, Chadwick's mother quizzed him and his two older brothers on what they were reading. She wanted to make sure they understood.

Chadwick looked up to his brother Kevin *(left)*.

Chadwick wanted to become a storyteller. While in **college**, he decided to study **directing**. He took acting classes to help improve his directing skills. Chadwick thought if he knew more about what actors did, it could make him a better director. Soon, he found that he wanted to be an actor, too!

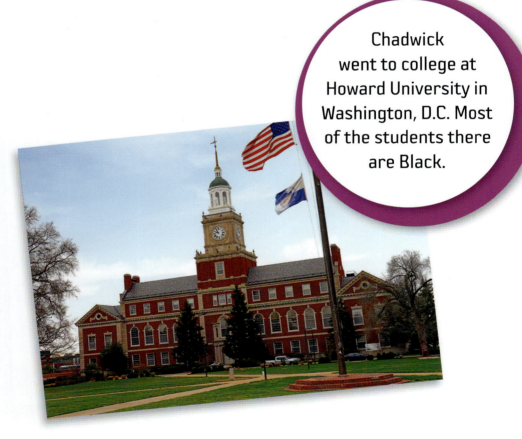

Chadwick went to college at Howard University in Washington, D.C. Most of the students there are Black.

In 2018, Chadwick spoke to students graduating from Howard University.

On-Screen Inspiration

In 2008, Chadwick moved to Los Angeles, California, to become an actor. But he was **disappointed** by the roles he was offered. Many of the parts for Black actors showed harmful **stereotypes**. Chadwick knew he wanted to play parts in stories that made him proud. He began to choose his roles carefully.

Chadwick turned down several small roles in TV shows while he was waiting for the right projects.

A lot of movies and TV shows are filmed in Los Angeles.

In 2013, Chadwick got his first big break. He played baseball player Jackie Robinson in the movie *42*. The movie made Chadwick a rising star. Soon, he got other roles playing **iconic** Black men. Chadwick played the singer and dancer James Brown in the movie *Get on Up*. He also took the part of activist and lawyer Thurgood Marshall in the movie *Marshall*.

Chadwick spent two months learning how to dance like James Brown for *Get on Up*.

42 is a movie about the first modern Black player in Major League Baseball.

As well as playing heroes from history, Chadwick became a superhero in the movie *Black Panther*. This was another opportunity for him to show Black people in a powerful way. His character T'Challa was the king of a fictional African country. Chadwick helped the film celebrate African culture. He wanted Black children to have a superhero that looked like them.

Chadwick *(middle)* with fellow *Captain America* stars Robert Downey Jr. *(left)* and Chris Evans *(right)*.

Chadwick first played the role of superhero T'Challa in the 2016 movie, *Captain America: Civil War*.

Chadwick fought for T'Challa to speak with an accent.

Off-Screen Superhero

Every role Chadwick chose supported his goal to show Black culture in a positive way. He found ways to support people off-screen, too. He spoke out in favor of the **Black Lives Matter** movement. And he helped raise millions of dollars for Black communities that were hit hard by COVID-19.

The Black Lives Matter movement focuses on the value of Black communities.

In June 2020, Chadwick and 300 other artists signed a letter asking Hollywood to find ways to better support Black artists.

Chadwick often went to events that supported causes he cared about.

In 2016, Chadwick learned he had **cancer**. But he didn't let this stop him from doing what he loved. He kept his illness a secret so fans would focus on his acting rather than his illness. He continued to act, speak out, and even visit sick kids in hospitals. Sadly, Chadwick died on August 28, 2020. Many fans were surprised and shared their support for the actor.

Chadwick wanted to be a role model for his fans.

Chadwick married Taylor Simone Ledward in 2020.

Celebrating Chadwick

Chadwick left a **legacy** that celebrates Black culture. He spent his life sharing powerful stories of heroes. He became a superhero off-screen, too. Because of his work, his memory will continue to inspire people to celebrate the importance of Black culture.

After Chadwick died, the college he went to named a building after him.

Chadwick Boseman • 1976–2020

Timeline

Here are some key dates in Chadwick Boseman's life.

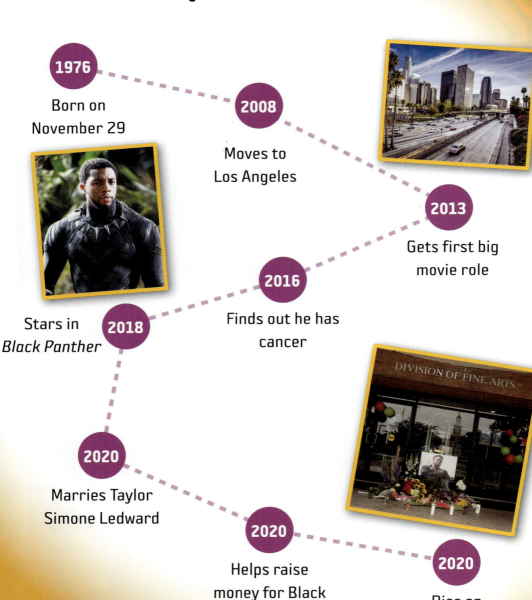

1976 — Born on November 29

2008 — Moves to Los Angeles

2013 — Gets first big movie role

2016 — Finds out he has cancer

2018 — Stars in *Black Panther*

2020 — Marries Taylor Simone Ledward

2020 — Helps raise money for Black communities hit by COVID-19

2020 — Dies on August 28

Glossary

Black Lives Matter an organization that seeks to end racism and empower Black individuals

cancer a serious, often deadly, disease

celebrate to do something special for important people or events

college a school people can go to after high school

directing telling actors what to do in a movie or play

disappointed made sad because something was not as good as you thought it might be

iconic something or someone that is well known

inspired encouraged to do things

legacy something left by a person in the past

premiere the first public showing of a movie

stereotypes sets of harmful ideas about how people from a specific group will behave

Index

Anderson, South Carolina 6
Black Lives Matter 16
Black Panther 4, 14, 22
Brown, James 12
cancer 18, 22
college 8, 20
COVID-19 16, 22
culture 4, 14, 16, 20
42 12-13
Get on Up 12
Marshall, Thurgood 12
Robinson, Jackie 12
stereotypes 10
superhero 4, 14, 16, 20

Read More

Borgert-Spaniol, Megan. *Chadwick Boseman: Acting Superstar (Superstars)*. Minneapolis: Abdo Publishing, 2021.

Huddleston, Emma. *Chadwick Boseman (Superhero Superstars)*. Lake Elmo, MN: Focus Readers, 2021.

Learn More Online

1. Go to **www.factsurfer.com** or scan the QR code below.
2. Enter "**Chadwick Boseman**" into the search box.
3. Click on the cover of this book to see a list of websites.

About the Author

Rachel Rose is a writer who lives in San Francisco. Her favorite books to write are about people who lead inspiring lives.